Letters from M

Garfield, aged about 22, as a junior engineer officer
of the White Star Line

DEAR GARF

LETTERS FROM MACHEN TO A SON AT SEA

Edited and annotated by
ARTHUR HERBERT JONES

First Impression - November 1991

© Arthur Herbert Jones

ISBN 0 86383 821 9

Printed in Wales by J. D. Lewis and Sons Ltd.,
Gomer Press, Llandysul

TO SONYA AND RUTH

CONTENTS

LIST OF ILLUSTRATIONS

INTRODUCTION

This book owes its appearance to the initiative and support of a fellow native of Machen, Bill Stephen, whose grandparents and parents I knew well, but Bill, born five years after I had left the village, I had never met. It came about in this way.

When, in 1973, my cousin Norman (Garfield's elder son) showed me his grandfather's letters and allowed me to take extracts, I had nothing more in mind than a vague wish to preserve some intensely interesting fragments of family and village history. (It was well I did so, as since Norman's death some months later the letters have disappeared.) A year or so later I found time to edit and comment on the letters from the vantage point of one who, born in the year before the first was written, knew most of the people named. Then, not knowing what to do with what I had written, I put the papers in a drawer and forgot about them. They would be there still had not Bill Stephen, who having read *His Lordship's Obedient Servant* and liked it, wrote telling me so and asking whether I had any other writings I could show him. I sent him my rough typescript, uncorrected and unrevised. Fascinated, as I had been, by its portrayal of day-to-day life in his native village almost a century ago, he urged me to consider offering the work for publication.

He felt, too, that the story might well be supplemented by a first-hand account of the conditions, social and religious, in which the incidents reported in the letters took place, and I responded by sending him a short essay, which I hoped he would approve. He did so, but his praise was tempered by some mild criticism. He thought I could do better and urged me to try again. Overcoming a feeling that approaching ninety I was back at my Risca grammar school of 75 years earlier, I wrote a piece double the length, which emerged as *Machen Revisited.* This earned pass marks.

11

Bill's career had begun as a ship's officer with the Radcliffe company of Cardiff, as had those of many other Machen men, some of whom are mentioned in the letters. Subsequently, he had embarked on an academic career, which, after university training had ended with his becoming Head of the Faculty of Education at Garnett College. With this background, combined with his knowledge of the village, his advice as a voluntary mentor had a value I could not ignore, and for which I'm profoundly grateful. He did more than encourage and advise: taking my badly typed scripts he put them through his word processor and returned them faultlessly finished. As if all this was not enough he then suggested that the work might be improved if furnished with a cast of characters and a family tree, both of which, with his help and that of others, named below I have been able to produce.

For that assistance I turned to another native of Machen, again one who had written to me after reading *His Lordship's Obedient Servant.* Doug. Thomas, son of a former much respected postmaster at Machen, after graduating from Swansea University, had, like Bill Stephen, taken up an academic career, from which he had just retired, and was willing to assist. I needed vital statistics of various members of the David Stephens family which involved research in the parish records. This, assisted by Raymond Cook, verger at St. John's Church, Doug. undertook and did well. He did much more: to him we owe the splendid photographs of Machen as it was in the years when the letters were written. To him also I am very grateful.

Others whom I wish to thank for help in various ways include: Sue Wetherill of Southampton, for permission to publish her grandfather's letters to her father and for providing photographs of them; Barbara Hallett of Westbury-on-Trym, a grand-daughter of David Stephens, for information about her father, David William Stephens, and his large family; Susan Ward of Broadstone, Dorset, a great-grand-daughter of David Stephens for the photo of Garfield and Laura with the principal guests at their wedding, and that of her grand-mother, 'Liz', and for information about the Davies branch of the family. Sidney Perkins of Barry, to whose annotated map of Bedwas and Machen, hanging on my study wall, I have frequently turned for confirmation of historic facts only dimly recalled; Dorothy Lennox of Killay, near Swansea, for information about her father, Hartwell Edmunds, and her mother, Rose (née Evans), Laura's sister.

I am also indebted to Margaret Stephen (née Oswell) formerly of Machen rectory, now of Fairford, Gloucestershire, for information about the Darby and Potter families.

These many acknowledgments demonstrate that this slim volume owes much to the interest and support of others, to all of whom I now offer my grateful thanks.

Lastly, I want to express my gratitude to Grace, my wife for more than sixty years, for her forbearance during the many hours this work kept me at my typewriter, the sound of which was never music to her ears!

August, 1991

CAST OF CHARACTERS

DAVID STEPHENS 1832-1906.

Described in the parish register on the occasion of Garfield's marriage as 'Superintendent of Tin (Tinplate) works (deceased)', an occupation he had followed both at Machen and in Brittany. At the time of writing the letters, 1903-06, he had retired. His wife, Susan, had died in 1899.

GARFIELD 1882-1947.

His youngest son. Born, and spent his early years, at Hennebont in Brittany. Spoke French fluently. Apprenticed engineer, Brecon and Merthyr Railway works at Machen. In 1903, aged 21, joined the White Star Line as an engineer. Passed his chief engineer's examination in 1908, aged 26. Served that company for about 42 years, mostly in their transatlantic liners, including R.M.S. Olympic (sister ship of the Titanic) and for much of that time as a Chief Engineer. Died in 1947, shortly after retiring, aged 65. On 4th. February 1909 married Laura Evans of Machen (q.v.).

LAURA 1883-1951. Garfield's wife.

Elder daughter of Thomas Evans, hotelier of Barking, Essex, who died in 1886, when she was three years old, and Isabella, daughter of James Potter, tinplate works manager of Machen.

Their children....

NORMAN 1910-1974.

Educated Machen Council School, Lewis's School, Pengam, King Edward 6th School, Southampton and Southampton University, B.Sc., A.M.I.C.E. Fellow of the Council of the Civil Engineers Institution. Unmarried.

15

SUSAN 1912- .

Married Alan Wetherill of Southampton, one son, one daughter.

JOAN 1917- .

Married George Hill of Southampton.

JOHN 1922-1982.

Served in Royal Air Force during World War 2. Personnel Manager, British American Tobacco Co. Ltd., Liverpool. Married Vivienne Hardy, one daughter, one son.

OTHER DESCENDANTS OF DAVID STEPHENS

ANITA (NETA).

Eldest daughter. Married Hancorn Tudor (Hank), a marine engineer. As he worked for lines based in Liverpool they made their home in that city. One son, three daughters.

ABRAM 1863-1919.

Eldest son. Steelworks manager at Piombino in Tuscany. Retiring early, he died at Machen, unmarried. Spoke Italian fluently, and obviously enjoyed doing so at Machen on his almost daily call for cigarettes at Berni's ice cream and soft drinks shop by the 'conker' tree. A charming, cheerful character and entertaining companion, well versed in local history.

JOHN 1865-1910.

An officer of the Cardiff Borough Police Force; promoted in March 1904 from Detective Sergeant to uniformed Inspector, died age 45, unmarried.

ELIZABETH ANN (LIZ) 1869-1932.

Married W. H. Davies ('W.H.') (1862-1911). Grocer and draper at Machen, also proprietor of a small colliery there. Lived with their seven children, next door to David

Stephens and his (then) unmarried daughter, Jane. Five daughters, all of whom married. Tragically, their two sons died young, Trevor in 1906, aged 11, and John in 1918, aged 25, unmarried. After David Stephens's death, W.H. was elected a County Councillor for Monmouthshire, and after his untimely death, aged 49, Elizabeth Ann, his widow, was appointed to the magistracy.

DAVID WILLIAM 1870-1937.

Third son, a marine engineer, serving during the currency of the letters mostly in Cardiff tramp steamers; later, on Dominion Line ships out of Bristol. In 1910, aged 40, married Janetta Pike, daughter of the licensee of the Hope and Anchor Inn at Shirehampton, near Avonmouth, then a country pub. Nine years later, with five small children, gave up his sea-going career to take over the license of the Inn and held it until his death in 1937, when it was taken over by his widow who held it for a further five years. Six sons and three daughters.

JANE 1876-1938. Married G. D. Inkin (1873-1955) q.v.

OTHER PRINCIPAL CHARACTERS

GRIFFITH D. INKIN 1873-1955.

Married David Stephens's youngest daughter, Jane, as his second wife. Schoolmaster at Machen for 27 years (1908-1935). Took a leading part in village and county activities. Urban District Councillor. Two sons by his first wife, Noel (manager of the National Westminster Bank at Reading and later at Cardiff) and Lloyd. Grandson, Colonel G.D.Inkin, O.B.E., D.L., formerly of the Royal Welch Fusiliers, currently (1991) chairman of the Cardiff Bay Development Corporation.

ERNEST MEYRICK (Ernest).

With his sister, Annie, and brother, Alfred, all three unmarried, grocer and baker at Machen, the business having been passed on to them by their father. Claimed descent from a well known Pembrokeshire family of that name. Staunch Wesleyan Methodist. Loved music; succeeded Laura, after her marriage, as organist at the local chapel. A member of the famous Royal Welsh Male Choir which in 1893 sang at the Chicago World Fair, and, on its return, before Queen Victoria at Windsor Castle. A genial and popular character with wide ranging interests.

HERBERT JONES 1845-1911.

Deputy Superintendent of the Brecon and Merthyr Railway, and manager of that company's workshops at Machen, where he trained Garfield and the other sea-going engineers mentioned in the Letters. Son of David Jones, civil engineer in charge of construction of that railway, circa 1865. Wife, Ann (1846-1936), daughter of James Potter (q.v.). Elder daughter, Mary, married Richard Martyn, another Machen grocer, before emigrating to the U.S.A. Younger daughter, Agnes (1864-1914) is mentioned in the Letters; she died unmarried. Elder son, Granville (1876-1960), father of the editor of these Letters. Younger son, Wyndham (1887-1940), trained under his father as an engineer and began his sea-going career on ships belonging to the Evan Thomas Radcliffe Company of Cardiff, but later joined the White Star Line and served on R.M.S. Olympic (under Garfield) and R.M.S. Majestic. On outbreak of war in 1939 joined Royal Navy and died by enemy action at sea the following year.

HARTWELL EDMUNDS (Hartie) 1883-1955.

A marine engineer trained at the local railway engineering works; joined the Evan Thomas Radcliffe Company of Cardiff and served on their ships for many years, for most of the time as a Chief Engineer; during first world war was on two of their ships sunk by German submarines. Married Rose Evans (1884-1967) Laura's younger sister. On retirement returned from Barry to Machen, where they died. One daughter, Dorothy, who married Gordon Lennox of Barry, pharmacist, later

Pharmaceutical Officer for the West Glamorgan Area of the National Health Service, M.B.E.

THE POTTER FAMILY

James Potter (1810-1887), wife ELIZABETH (1810-1877), came to Machen in the 1830s to take up a managerial post in the tinplate works owned by the Woodruff family. Two sons, four daughters. His daughter Ann (1846-1936) married Herbert Jones(q.v.). His daughter Isabella (born 1851) married Thomas Evans, parents of Laura and Rose (Edmunds). His elder son John (born 1835) owned the drapery business at Manchester House, and his daughters Emily and Rose, and son, Ted, are mentioned in the Letters. His daughter, Edith, a teacher, married another marine engineer, Harry Davies. A much respected and influential Machen family.

David Stephens (1832–1906) m. Sus

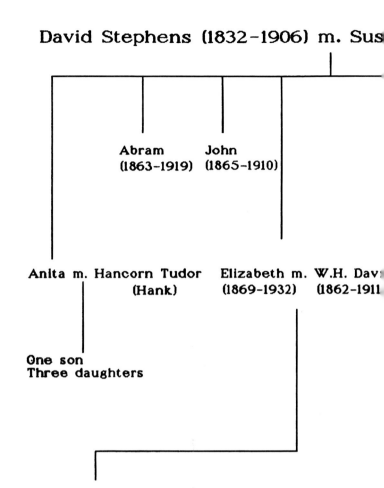

Abram   John
(1863–1919)   (1865–1910)

Anita m. Hancorn Tudor   Elizabeth m. W.H. Dav
          (Hank)   (1869–1932)   (1862–1911

One son
Three daughters

Clara (1890–1972) m. Dennis Morgan, two daughters
Ivy (1892–1976) m. Thomas Owen, one son, one daughter
John (1893–1918)
Trevor Garnot (1894–1906)
Evelyn (1895–1978) m. Melvyn Rees, two daughters
Rosalie (1897–1983) m. Dr. Ivor Morgan
Anita (1900–   ) m. Dr. Cecil Davies, two sons

Jane m. G.D. Inkin
(1876-1938) (1873-1955)

Garfield m. Laura Evans
(1882-1947) (1883-1951)

)avid William m. Janetta Pike
l870-1937) (1882-1967)

Norman (1910-1974)
Susan (1912-)m. E. A. Wetherill
    (1911-1991), one son, one daughter
Joan (1917-) m. George Hill
John (1922-1982) m. Vivienne Hardy,
    one daughter, one son.

hn George (1911-1965)
zabeth Mary (1912-1990)
vid (1914-1989) m. Gillian Metson, two sons
chard Lloyd (1916-1990)
arry Abram (1919-1978) m. Rosalene
    Buchanan, two sons
ter Colyn (1921-1934)
netta Barbara (1922-) m. Anthony
    Hallett, two daughters
cely (1924-) m. Barrie Morris, two sons
ecil (1924-) m. Sally Clarke, one daughter, one son.

21

Garfield with his father and mother outside their home in Brittany,
c. 1890

DEAR GARF

Some thirtyfive years ago—this is being written in 1984—an uncle of mine by marriage died at his home at Southampton shortly after beginning his retirement. His passing was untimely for of his sixty or so years more than forty had been spent at sea and he had earned some years of quiet enjoyment of home and family. On his decease his elder son discovered a pocket wallet that his father had carried with him throughout the whole of his sea-going career and in it a tight packet of old letters. They were not love letters from the girl his father married a few years after the last of them was written but letters from his grandfather to his father in the first few years of the latter's sea-going career. Such letters are seldom kept more than a few days and my cousin wondered what had made them so precious to his father that he had carried them over the seas of half the world through many hard and hazardous years, including those of both World Wars.

When shown to me I think I saw why they had been retained and treasured: they had given him what even photographs could not do—a succession of vivid glimpses of what his family, friends and neighbours were doing, their hopes and fears, their successes and failures, their crimes and punishments. Re-reading them in long absences in strange waters or among strange peoples he would have seen also his very happy home and even the mountain, fields and woods of his village exactly as they were. To-day, they have a wider interest for they show in a much changed Wales the family loyalties, 'the trivial round and common tasks' and the claims of firmly held religious belief and clearly seen moral values that obtained in a Welsh village eighty years ago.

With the permission of the surviving children of the man to whom they were addressed and who kept them so long, I am allowed to quote from them.

All were written between September 1903 and January 1906 by a man who was seventy when the correspondence

David Stephens when aged about 70.

Susannah Stephens, Garfield's mother.

began, the son being then about twenty, having just completed an engineering apprenticeship in workshops near his home in Machen, a village at the southern end of the Rhymney Valley in Gwent.

In 1912, when I was a boy of ten, Machen was, on the whole, a thriving as well as a beautiful village. As villages go, I now think that it was unique, not only because of its delightful setting below a nicely rounded mountain, clad with bracken and heather, its inviting woods, clear streams and well-kept upland and lowland farms, but also because it was the home of a number of small industries that gave employment to men with various skills who came there from all parts of the country, bringing with them habits and accents that made for an interesting, and, at times, a lively and amusing mix. It was a place that attracted and encouraged a number of men and women who refused to be cast in the common mould and, defying convention, were accepted as 'characters'.

In the years when the letters were written, the village had within it, or on its outskirts, two small drifts (coal mines), a woollen factory with its Welsh weavers, a tinplate works, brickworks, a sandstone quarry, a limestone quarry, a small but very active foundry and the engineering workshops of the Brecon and Merthyr Railway. It was the presence there of these workshops that accounts for Machen's close connection with the sea and ships, which figure so largely in the letters. In those workshops, under the supervision of my grandfather, Herbert Jones, not only Machen boys but also a number from other parts of South Wales received a thorough training as engineers. It was here the young man to whom the letters were sent had been trained to become a sea-going engineer. Machen trained men had earned a good reputation with the Engineering Superintendents of Cardiff shipowning companies and in the early years of this century they were sending home picture post-cards from ports all over the world, so that names such as Genoa, Naples, Patras, Port Said, Odessa, Bombay, Buenos Aires, Boston and New York were more familiar to me than towns in Wales. Most served in tramp steamers, a few on liners, among them the young man whose early years at sea were blessed by the love and unfailing interest in his well-being of the father who wrote those treasured letters.

The letters were meant to inform and this they did perfectly, although, in places, with a splendid disregard for grammar. Not that the writer was ill educated: by the standards of those days he was well educated, having spent a number of years in France in response to an invitation to take up a managerial post at a tinplate works at Hennebont in Brittany. Both father and son were French-speaking and, as the letters reveal, the old man was extremely knowledgeable, with wide ranging interests. Without doubt , he was a fine character, a patriarchal figure, the widower head of a family of many children, all of whom did well, the recipient being the youngest.

So a few days after his leaving home for Liverpool to begin what was to be a very long and very successful career as an engineer with the White Star Line the father wrote:

Wednesday, September 10th. 1903. Just a line before you leave. . . I suppose you are leaving in the Commonwealth tomorrow or you would have informed me. It being half holiday in the shop (the writer kept a general store specialising in ironmongery and china) Jane (a daughter) and Laura are gone over to Rhydygwern for blackberries and Liz, W.H., Clara and baby (daughter, son-in-law and two children) are gone in their trap to Newport and Abram (another son, a bachelor) is gone to Cardiff to see Goodfellow the lawyer re. purchasing Doctor's Row (a row of cottages). They are for sale and I intend offering £550 to £600 for them. . .

Rankin (a detective with the Cardiff Police) is going to Canada to Montreal, by the Southwark, to fetch a prisoner home, a young girl from Cardiff who had embezzled £200 from her employers money. . .

John Holman and his wife are very poorly. The doctors say that Mrs. Holman won't live more than two or three months. I have been very near the top of

27

the mountain this morning and feel a little tired now so Jane must finish this when she comes home.

(Jane does so). I see father has left space for me to write to you but goodness knows what I have to write about. I have just been gathering blackberries with Laura. I got three pints so look out for tarts now. Don't you wish you were nearer. . .?

Garnet Everson and the chip-shop girl are to be married next week—Monday—and Sid is best man and Nellie I hear is bridesmaid. They are getting married in Stow Hill Wesleyan chapel. . .

Herbert Darby is coming to Machen some day this week. You know the one that was engaged to Rose Potter. I don't know if they will make it up or not. Ted Potter is coming home next week, for good I believe. Thanks very much for list of sailings. It will be very useful. Do you think the Commonwealth will go to the Mediterranean? Your affectionate sister, Jane.

Having regard for all the circumstances I cannot imagine any letter having greater interest for the young engineer leaving home for the first time. Laura, who with Jane, went picking blackberries was the young woman who, some seven or eight years later, he was to marry and I have no doubt they were in love with each other at the time that he left home. The scene the words evoke is one of bucolic peace and beauty: the two handsome young women (and to their beauty I can warmly testify) blackberry picking at Rhydygwern, a farm on the 'other side' of the river with a panoramic view of the village on the slopes opposite, backed by the mountain then fully clothed in bracken and heather, followed by the mouth-watering prospect of blackberry tart for tea!

Things are different now. The emancipated young women of today have opted for work in office or factory, travelling there and back by car or bus, and by choice or necessity buying their fruits in cans from the supermarkets on a weekly foraging expedition. And that is what we mean by progress.

Commercial Road, Machen, circa. 1960, drawn by Cyrus Hughes, showing the bay-windowed house on extreme left, the home of Laura Evans prior to her marriage to Garfield.

And how many men of seventy now find pleasure in climbing 'very near the top' of Mynydd Machen? Or how many of twenty do so? A few years ago, on revisiting the village, I discovered that one can be taken by car to a spot near the 800 ft.contour line and that, it seems, is the preferred method of climbing, as the main mountain path, over which I walked daily to and from school at Risca for three years during the first World War, shows few signs of current use and for a long stretch has disappeared altogether. That mountain top offers marvellous views over the Bristol Channel towards Somerset, clean mountain air and in summer the song of skylarks, but the preferred choice is the seaside at Barry or by motorway to Bristol or Bath if the attractions of Cardiff have begun to pall.

Machen, in 1902, had a population of fewer than two thousand, yet what a lot of news of comings and goings, of crime, of sickness, of a marriage planned, and of an engagement in jeopardy, and of an important business deal contemplated—all packed succinctly into that relatively short letter from which I have made only a few small excisions!

Of John Holman and his wife who 'are very poorly' there will be more in later letters.

Herbert Darby, whose coming is expected within a week, was the eldest son of the Rev. J. C. S. Darby, M.A., rector of Machen from 1873 to c. 1901, a man of some standing socially, who, when an elderly widower with three sons had married Emily Potter, a daughter of John Potter of Manchester House, Machen. Emily was said to be younger than any of the rector's sons, Herbert, Fred and Harry, and she presented him with a fourth, William Augustus. 'Bilgus', as he was affectionately known in the village, died young: he was killed early in the first world war while serving as an officer in the Monmouthshire Regiment, leaving Emily both widowed and childless. I remember her as a kind and gentle woman, who seemed to accept with Christian fortitude and serenity the sorrows that had befallen her and the hard times that came with them. Leaving Machen in 1921 and Wales in 1934, I lost touch with her and seventy years later it has pleased me to hear that her stepson, Harry, returning to the village after having done well as a rubber planter in Malaya, had taken his aged step-mother into his delightful home, Bovil House, there to dwell in ease until his own death a few years later.

And now, in September 1903, Herbert, whose engagement to Rose Potter, one of Emily's younger sisters, had recently been broken off, was revisiting the village, giving rise to speculation as to whether the broken-off engagement would be renewed. It was not, and Rose died unmarried only a few years later. Her death was followed within a year or so, as I recall, by that of her sister and near neighbour, Clara, who left three young children, among them my friend Jack Rees. Ted Potter, their brother, was a Captain in the Salvation Army in Ceylon (as Sri Lanka was then known) and we shall be hearing more about him.

Garnet Everson who was about to be married to the chip-shop girl is not mentioned in subsequent letters and I will speak of him now. He was a much liked and respected young man in Machen in those days and I remember him with admiration and affection, but as with so many other Welshmen of my acquaintance he was a victim of his fiery temperament. He was a miner at Nine Mile Point Colliery over the mountain in the Sirhowy valley, a three-mile trudge morning and night by a stony path over a bleakly exposed mountain with a further long walk underground to and from the coal-face. Naturally, he was strong and healthy, and clean looking withal, with strong yet pleasant features, black hair and eyes indicative of his honest and fearless nature. And he had a fine bass voice that he used with advantage both in the Wesleyan chapel and in open air meetings where he showed himself to be a natural orator. Had he been better educated and enjoyed the advantages that were to follow even in the early years of my lifetime I would have foretold a successful career for him as a socialist politician.

Thirteen years after his marriage to the chip-shop girl, that is in the summer of 1915, when I suppose he was in his late thirties, I then thirteen, remember his speaking at an open-air recruiting meeting in the village. A recruiting sergeant for the Army had come from Newport, hoping to win recruits and a fair number of people of all ages had assembled in the school yard to hear what our schoolmaster, Mr. Inkin, and Garnet Everson had to say. Mr. Inkin was capable of making a good speech at all times and no doubt did so on this occasion but he made no lasting impression on me—possibly because I had heard his voice too often! But when Garnet spoke, the passion and eloquence of this unlettered man stirred me deeply. Had I been old enough the army would have had another recruit that evening! As it was, a number of youths responded to the call to serve and marched off behind the sergeant to the Fwrrwn Ishta inn, there to take the King's shilling. On the way home from the meeting I was overtaken by a woman running and sobbing as she ran. 'What's the matter Mrs. Vines?' I asked. 'I hear Alf has gone to enlist and I want to stop him' and she ran on. She was too late, Alf, with others, had enlisted, but survived the war as his name does not appear among those listed as killed on the village War Memorial.

Four years later, that is in 1919, a troubled Garnet knocked on the door of my paternal grandmother, also a Methodist. 'I've come to say goodbye, Mrs. Jones'. 'Goodbye! Whatever for, Garnet?', asked grandmother. 'I'm going to America in the morning. Had a row with the manager, lost my temper and threatened to throw him down the pit. And now he's taking out a summons against me.' Knowing Garnet and remembering his temper and his great physical strength I believe he had done more than just threaten—that he had taken hold of the manager by the throat.

He went to America and it now strikes me as amazing that seventy years ago one could go off just like that—by taking a train to Liverpool and with no more than twenty-five pounds in one's pocket and without visa or passport take ship for America. This tale should end with 'and he lived happily ever after.' A few years after his sudden leave-taking he turned up almost penniless and seemingly defeated at the home of an aunt of mine at Cleveland,

Ohio. The American colliery bosses in those days were apparently much tougher than their Welsh counterparts and Garnet was no match for men with guns.*

The next letter is dated January 15th. 1904, that is, four months later. After titbits of news about the family the old man turns to news of three men who had been fellow apprentices with the son at the local railway works.

> Wm. Smith has not been for his exam yet. He is going in a fortnight so he says. He has taken to drink and has a very foul mouth. Wm. Hill was here yesterday saying that he has tried all the shipping firms that he knows and always the same reply, not wanted. He was saying how lucky you had been to get into the White Star Line. Jack the Mill is home too. He has the promise of a boat in about six weeks.
>
> Poor John Holman is gone—burying him tomorrow (this is the man, who, with his wife, was reported as 'very poorly' four months earlier and there are further references to this tragic family later).

And it ends with this patriarchal blessing -

> Take care of yourself and may God bless and protect you from all harm. Much love from all. Father.

The next letter was written some six weeks later, that is on February 25th. 1904. Before quoting from it I should explain that Garfield, the son to whom the letters were sent, was now a very junior engineer on the White Star Liner Canopic, then employed on the Genoa-Naples and Boston, U.S.A. run and that his brother Abram, who had been home on leave at Machen when Garfield left to go to sea had returned to his job as a manager at a large steelworks at Piombino, a coastal town opposite the island of Elba in northern Italy. These Christian names, Garfield and Abram (not Abraham), were unusual in Wales at that time, and have not become popular since. I believe Garfield was named after President James Abram Garfield of the United States who had been cruelly assassinated

---

* I have since learned that he later 'made good' in Detroit where he was employed in the motor industry.

White Star Liner Canopic on which Garfield served in 1904. Reproduced by permission of the National Maritime Museum, London.

after holding that office for only a few months in 1881, that is, a year or so before he was born. President Garfield was the sort of man the father would honour and respect—of humble birth he had, by diligence in study and work, and by bravery in battle risen to the top. The letter begins:

> Your very welcome letter to hand this morning. . . I hope you received the last letter I wrote to Naples. . . We got a very interesting letter from Abram giving us a beautiful description of the Canopic as she passed by Piombino. He and many more of his friends had been watching for a long time before she hove in sight and they watched till she was no more to be seen.

I should explain, perhaps, that Piombino is set on a promontory. The letter proceeds:

> In his letter (that is Abram's) he says on Carnival night when all the people were in the height of their festival (presumably a Shrove Tuesday festival) a French schooner was wrecked close in sight not 50 yards from the shore, and the six men on board were washed up at their feet, four of them living and two dead. They were from the island of Corsica. . .
>
> It gave me great pleasure to see that you were enjoying yourself in looking at Naples from the bay and viewing the much talked of Vesuvius.

There follows news of his friends and acquaintances.

> William Hill and Smith are still idle. I hear that Jack the Mill has a boat to go to next week. John Arthur Thomas (Keeper's son) had an accident Tuesday night at Rudry colliery. The rope broke letting a full journey of trams run back into the drift. Him and a young man from Rudry were hurt but not seriously. I am pleased to tell you I am much better these last few days. Yesterday I went so far as Machen Village (Lower Machen) and I go backwards and forwards to Abram's houses every day. I suppose I am his estate agent. They are nearly finished.
>
> I find from the newspapers today that there are very important changes in the White Star Company.

Bruce Ismay is gone from Liverpool to New York to take (over) the sole management of the combine and that he is going to put the Marconi telegraph on all their boats. Are you aware that Hank is put chief of the Vancouver and that she is laid up but he gets full pay.

The school inspector was in the boys' school one day this week so he put the boys to write a letter. John Davies's letter (John, a grandson aged eleven, lived in Russell House, next door) was to his uncle Garf. and in it he said he was going to run up to Liverpool to see you on 31st. February, so the inspector read it and asked when is John Davies going to see his uncle so they all shouted never. John then saw his mistake.

I hope you are reading Read's or some other work on engineering... If you wish me to get you one let me know...

Clara (a grand-daughter eldest of Elizabeth's five daughters) has had two cards from you—views of the theatre and The Square, Naples.

It was that move by the White Star Line to install the Marconi telegraph, which we knew as wireless telegraphy, that contributed to the saving of many lives when their Titanic was sunk some six years later.

A further six weeks and another letter. In the previous letter he had said that 'Jack the Mill has a boat to go to next week'. He now reports that Jack the Mill's boat had been lost near Bizerta in Tunisia—all hands saved. He adds 'Now there is another Cardiff boat gone down near the same place'. It is obvious that service on board Cardiff tramp steamers in those days was a fairly hazardous occupation. There follow snippets of village news. Mrs. Davies (W.H's mother) and old Mrs. Griffin had died. 'Williams the preacher is selling Evan Jones's house by auction tomorrow in Newport ... Mr. Johns is going to build a house in the Fwrrwm field for Dr. Barnard ...William Hill (the engineer who had been reported idle—in modern parlance that means unemployed) is home again' which suggests that he had secured a berth on a ship but only for a short time.

Then the father asks: 'Have any of your married men been relieved or are you all going to stick to her as long as she is in that trade?'. This throws light on the conditions of service at sea in those days. The Canopic, as I have said, was operating between Genoa and Boston, calling at Naples, and even the married engineering officers accepted the possibility, as an obligation of their calling, that if the shipowners did not recall the ship to the United Kingdom for repairs or for another trade route they would remain with her, for years on end if necessary. And I have noted that in the two years and four months covered by the letters there is no reference to Garfield having been home, although there is a suggestion in one letter that one or more members of his family were prepared to go up to Liverpool to see him when the ship called at that port.

The letter ends on a homely note. 'If you did come home for a short time I could find you some work making chicken houses. They are getting quite dilapidated the old ones. We have a very fine lot of fowls, Orpingtons, Longshanks and Minorcas'. That reminds me that many households at Machen kept chickens if they had gardens big enough, and not a few kept pigs. And the names mentioned— Orpingtons, Longshanks and Minorcas—suggest, and my memory confirms, they were chosen as much for their fine appearance as for their egg-laying performance or as table birds.

On May 13th. 1904, the father wrote again and his opening sentence throws further light on conditions in those days. This time on the postal service. The mail arrived at Machen at 8.55 and on week-days there were deliveries at about 9.30 and 4.30 and one on Sundays. The letter begins:

> We have been expecting a letter from Naples but it has not arrived yet and to-morrow will be the last day we can expect to have one for I see by the papers that you have left since the 11th. for Boston.

On the 13th. he was confidently expecting a letter that he

assumed had been posted on or before the 11th and was confident that if there was none on the morrow there wouldn't be one at all. Two days, or three at the most, between Naples and Machen! Such was the postal service at that time. Nowadays, served by air, we feel lucky if we can get one from Italy in a week!

He goes on to say, 'Liz (a married daughter living next door) and I went for a drive on Wednesday afternoon around Rudry and Caerphilly.' The conveyance was, of course, a horse and carriage, almost certainly a dog cart or governess cart. And what went they forth to see? Probably nothing in particular but to enjoy the fresh air and the unspoiled countryside of those days as he says 'the country is looking splendid now with primroses, cowslips and kingcups.'

And again references to ships and the men and boys of Machen serving in them:

> As I was passing the Post Office yesterday William Edwards called after me and told me that Gwyn is gone in the Vancouver with Hank as electrician. (He believed Hank had got him in)... they are sailing from Liverpool to Montreal.

Mr. Edwards was the village postmaster, and a minor composer, whose bardic name was Gwilym Lôn. Gwyn was a son of his and Hank, who had got him work on the Vancouver, was a son-in-law of the writer.

He further reports that 'Ted Potter is home for a few weeks. He is not very well.' This is the Salvation Army officer home from service in Ceylon. Thus day after day Machen is shown to be a place not only of much natural beauty but also a village from which men were constantly departing for far distant lands and returning with strange tales to tell. It was, as I remember it, and these letters confirm, a world conscious, outward-looking community, with no time for boredom.

The next letter, dated June 18th 1904, abounds with such references. It begins:

> We received your postcard yesterday and you promised that we would have a letter today but it has

Herbert Jones, Deputy Superintendent of the Brecon and Merthyr Railway, who trained the many marine engineers mentioned in the Letters. Grandfather of Arthur Herbert Jones who edited them.

not arrived. (Obviously Garfield was as dutiful as his father in writing regularly.) Very likely it will be here in the morning. (Again, absolute confidence in the international postal service!) I hear that Laura (Garfield's acknowledged sweetheart at this time and future wife) had a souvenir by this post . . .

I am very proud to know that you are having such a pleasant experience of seafaring and not in one of those coal hulks (a reference to Cardiff tramp steamers, especially those on the South Wales to Port Said and/or Odessa run, which was the main trade route of some companies). I'm afraid our David William has injured his health by being in them . . . (David William was another marine-engineer son). Of course you know that Hartie (Edmunds) is gone with Edgar Davies to sea. . . I don't know what grade he is or Edgar . . .

These two, Hartie (Hartwell) Edmunds and Edgar Davies were also marine engineers. Hartie, aged 21, had just completed his apprenticeship, and, like so many of his fellow apprentices, was beginning his sea-going career with the Evan Thomas Radcliffe Company of Cardiff, with whom he remained for many years, for most of them as chief engineer. He is of special interest in this story as in 1915, six years after Garfield's marriage to Laura Evans, he married Laura's sister, Rose, and after living for some years at Barry, they returned to Machen to retire, and die. Of some interest also were his experiences during the first world war. When that war began he was chief engineer on Radcliffe's S.S. Patagonia, then on a voyage to Odessa for grain after delivering coal to a Mediterranean port. With the entry of Turkey into the war the Patagonia was trapped in the Black Sea, where, on 15th September 1915 it was sunk by a German submarine. Hartie, with the rest of the crew, was rescued, and their long journey home began by train across Russia from Odessa to Archangel. Undeterred, he returned to sea and was again on a merchant ship sunk by submarine, this time in the

Mediterranean. Again, he was rescued and on this occasion had not to swim for it as on the first.

To return to the letter of June 18th 1904: 'Jack the Mill has been home for some time but I hear he is going away next week.' (His shipwreck off Bizerta had not daunted him, and, remembering the man, I'm not surprised. He was always cheerful, gentle and kind in his ways and immensely popular—a man greatly respected.)The letter continues: 'Will Hill has been home this week. He is the same as usual. He brought a Spanish fireman with him to carry his luggage home.' This is the Will Hill who in the previous autumn could not find a job—at least at sea.

The letter ends on a comforting note, again with a patriarchal touch. 'I am pleased to tell you that we are all well and financially we are better off than ever so when we look round we have much cause for thankfulness in the way the Lord has and is blessing us as a family'.

And the next letter, written three months later, that is on October 15th, 1904, portrays an event in which members of his family took part, with no small credit. It is, also, an occasion typical of many in those days in the South Wales valleys where entertainment was home-made, innocent and edifying:

> Did I tell you in my letter to Boston of the tea party and concert we had in our chapel on Monday last? W.H. (the grocer son-in-law) had the providing of the tea and at the concert we had two ladies from Bassaleg, Ernest, Eddie. Mrs. Willie Beeston and her sister-in-law sang a duet but it was all a rather tame affair until the two Miss. Davieses, Rosalie and Eveline, were called to sing a duet which fairly brought the house down, encored with tremendous applause. It really was the song of the evening. Clara accompanied them, but Laura was accompanist of the evening.

Rosalie and Eveline and Clara who 'accompanied them' were three of the five daughters of W.H. and therefore the writer's grandchildren. At that time Rosalie and Eveline could not have been more than ten years of age. I

41

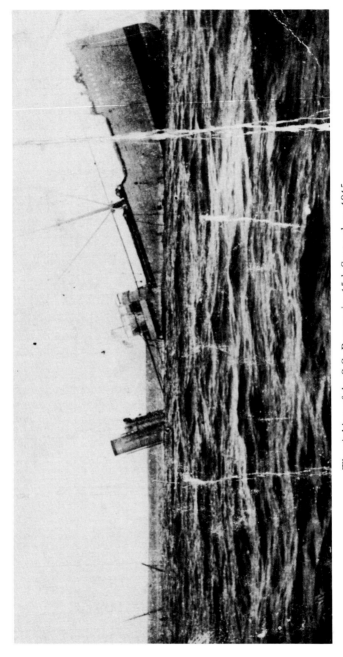

The sinking of the S.S. Patagonia, 15th September, 1915.
(Reproduced by permission of the Welsh Industrial & Maritime Museum, Cardiff.)

S. S. Wimborne, belonging to Evan Thomas Radcliffe & Co., Cardiff, a typical Cardiff tramp steamer of those years. On her first three voyages, 1911-12, two of her four engineers were Machen trained, Hartwell Edmunds (mentioned in the Letters), and Wyndham Jones.

(Reproduced by permission of the Welsh Industrial & Maritime Museum, Cardiff.)

remember them as exquisitely pretty girls, a few years older than I. Laura, as mentioned earlier, was Garfield's sweetheart. Another in the cast is worthy of notice. Ernest was Ernest Meyrick, another grocer, who played the organ and led the singing in the Wesleyan Methodist Chapel. He had a splendid bass voice and some years earlier had been a member of the Royal Welsh Male Voice Choir that had toured in Canada and the United States, and, on its return to this country, had been commanded to sing before Queen Victoria at Windsor Castle, as a large photograph in his dining room showing the large choir before the castle eloquently testified. He was a popular character in the village, whose stories about his experiences in America never failed to enthral me.

And on to more mundane matters:

> I have been to Newport to-day—at the bank for Abram and myself. Crowds going by train as the notorious Dai the Mill was summoned for being drunk and disorderly and only last week he had to pay £2...I made a mistake it was for refusing to quit the Tredegar Arms. I don't know what it cost him....

By 1912, that is some eight years later, Dai the Mill must have quit the scene as I can't remember him. Was he, I wonder, a brother to Jack the Mill? In that case their characters were vastly different.

And then back to matters spiritual. 'I am very pleased to hear that you enjoyed yourself so much on Sunday at the Tremont Temple. We are having Mark Guy Pearce here in a fortnight. Preach in the afternoon and lecture at night at Siloam.'

Again, a vivid glimpse into the habits and pleasures of the men and women of Machen (or at least some of them) eighty years ago. In the two or three days that his ship was at Boston the young engineer had found time to attend a service at the Tremont Temple, a large, and to those interested, world famous Nonconformist Chapel, and had been happy to do so.

Mark Guy Pearce was a popular Wesleyan Methodist preacher and lecturer, based in London. He would have preached at the small Methodist chapel but for the popular lecture the largest of the four Nonconformist chapels was used. He was still revisiting Machen for such purposes— religious and cultural (certainly not political)—during my boyhood there and his sayings were often quoted in my hearing. I believe the lectures were on a professional basis, inasmuch as he was paid for them, usually by what was known as a 'silver collection'.

Visiting preachers and lecturers, the latter often aided by a magic lantern, were assured of a warm welcome and appreciative congregations or audiences. They did much to reduce the risk of insularity and contributed not a little to the interest shown by the men and women of the place in matters outside their natural orbits.

Other days, other ways! To-day I suppose a visiting lecturer, other than a ranting politician, would not half-fill the smallest of the four Nonconformist chapels that served the village when I lived there. Indeed, of those four chapels, only the smallest, Ebenezer, is left. Though the place has apparently doubled in size the Methodist chapel, Adullam for the Congregationalists and the larger of the two Baptist chapels, Siloam, all have died of neglect and in the case of the two last mentioned the places on which they stood know them no more. And how many young Welshmen of to-day, spending a week-end at Boston, Massachusetts, would make for the Tremont Temple? In those deserted and destroyed chapels we had been taught—and some of us came to accept—that in the words of John Newton's famous hymn:

> Fading is the worldling's pleasure,
> All his boasted pomp and show;
> Solid joys and lasting treasure
> None but Zion's children know.

Four days later, that is on October 19th. 1904, the dutiful father writes again. After reporting that a son* then living in Cardiff had 'come in for the day' and that he had seen in the papers that a ship, the Oxonian, on which

* John, then an inspector in the Cardiff Borough Police.

another son, David William, was serving, had passed the Lizard bound for Montreal, he reports:

> They are all alive here to-day over going in to Cardiff to hear Torrey and Alexander. W.H. (a son-in-law) has a brake full of Wesleyans—men— and Liz (the writer's daughter and wife of W.H.) is taking their own carriage with Jane, Agnes, Laura, Rose and herself. They are starting from here at 5 p.m. catch a train at Caerphilly and the conveyances are to remain at Caerphilly until they return . . .

I can guess the identities of a number of the men in the brake, but I knew well the five young ladies in the carriage and even in my young and untutored eyes they were gay and comely, even beautiful and I still have photographs to confirm my boyhood impressions.

Torrey and Alexander were American evangelists, as were Moody and Sankey, who preached and sang very much in the style of Billy Graham.

The letter goes on to report a spiritual disaster.

> I suppose you have heard by the papers of the great fraud David Shepherd, robbing the school of £6,000 and about £6,000 from the Star Bowkit Society. Of course you know he is (or was) one of the leading Wesleyans in Cardiff and one of the leading men in the Free Church Council. Now he is in Cardiff jail.

I was less than three years old when this was happening but years later my father often mentioned the shock and distress felt by Wesleyan Methodists in South Wales by the disgrace that had fallen upon one of their most respected leaders. David Shepherd was an accountant. I was glad to see some twentyfive years later that his son had become and remained a leading and much respected figure in Cardiff society: he had not allowed his father's fall to get him down and that demanded courage of a high order.

The next letter, two months later, that is on December 8th 1904, is packed with news that must have been of absorbing interest to the son, whose appreciation can be assessed by the fact that he treasured it, along with the others over so many years. The son's ship was then at Genoa and the father begins by expressing pleasure that the son, Garfield, intended to visit his brother Abram, at Piombino, roughly 150 miles distant, on the following Sunday.

He then reports the big news of the week for Machen people: Evan Roberts, the great Welsh revivalist, had come to the village and was conducting mission services in one of its chapels that, twenty years later were recalled with wonder, for some 'who came to scoff, remained to pray.' The writer refers to the mission in these words:

> I dare say you will get all the news of the great revival that is taking place in Wales...It is marvellous to hear the conversions that are taking place all over the country. Jane and David William have just come in from chapel, 10p.m.,and last night there was 15 young men, chiefly apprentices, came out to be on the Lord's side.
>
> Ted Potter is here for a week or so before leaving for Ceylon again as captain in the Salvation Army. We have all had postcards from Hank at New Orleans to-day. He expects to be in Liverpool on 16th. Gwyn (Edwards) is still here. He was enquiring after you. Going to sea has very much improved him both in appearance and manners. D. Wm. (David William) will give you a report of his experiences in the Oxonian... Old Ed. Rogers is in the hands of his creditors. He has been here this morning. He wants me to buy his houses. I am offering him £380 for them. I believe I shall have them. Sat. (the following day). I am going into Newport with him now by the 12.20.

(The rest of the letter is in another's handwriting.)

> It is the property by the Reading Room, Richardson's, J. Heaths and the chapel that father means.
>
> I have been offered another second berth, possibly in the Anglian about Christmas time so I am here

Garfield and Laura with the principal guests at their wedding, 4th February, 1909.

AT THE WEDDING OF GARFIELD AND LAURA.

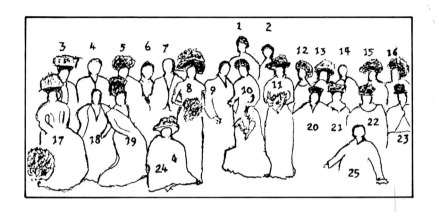

1. Mrs Osmond-Barnard and   2. her sister

3. Mrs. Granville Jones (mother of the editor of these letters)

4. Herbert Jones 5.   6. W.H. Davies ("W.H.")

7. David William Stephens, Best Man

8. Miss Rose Evans, Laura's sister, Bridesmaid

9. Garfield 10. Laura

11. Miss Jane Stephens, Garfield's sister, Bridesmaid

12. Miss Annie Meyrick   13. Miss Rose Potter

14. Dr. Osmond-Barnard

15. Miss Edith Potter 16. Mrs. Clara Rees (née Potter)

17. Miss Agnes Jones, Laura's cousin

18 Mrs. Herbert Jones, Laura's aunt   19 Mrs W.H. Davies ("Liz")

20. Mrs. Thomas Evans, Laura's mother. 21.

22. Mrs. John Potter, and 23. John Potter, Laura's uncle

24. & 25. Ivy and John Davies, daughter and son of "W.H." and "Liz",
niece and nephew of Garfield.

awaiting orders. Everybody here is all right but miserable weather since I am home. We are looking forward to Abram coming home next week. Dave (David William).

Writing again six days later, that is, on the 14th. December 1904, he reports that the religious enthusiasm inspired by Evan Roberts had not died down and cites a prayer meeting that was being held in Ebenezer chapel that Wednesday morning. The letter begins:-

Abram has just come home by the first train having slept at Newport. Well I am pleased you were together for a short time at Genoa. He has just opened his bags and you can guess the excitement with the children next door (five girls and two boys). I am very pleased with the chest preserver. I have no doubt it is a very good thing. . . .

Of course you have had all the news from Abram. . . Now I have to thank you for the greenbacks you sent me for £75. I will take care of it for you so whenever you need it you know where to find it.

You will be glad to hear that I have bought Capel-y-Groes property. . .I went to Newport yesterday and bought it for £390, they paying for the transfer . . .I have room to build another house on the ground at £5. a year for the whole, so yesterday was quite a red letter day with us as last night was the first time for me to be on the Parish Council

Industrial matters are also mentioned. His grocer son-in-law, W.H., had become a colliery proprietor in a very modest way, having opened up a drift coal mine in a wood in the village, employing ten men. 'You will be glad to hear that W.H. has got a splendid seam of coal in the Fedw, 5 feet thick and still improving. He expects great things there now. . .'. That was in 1904; I remember the undertaking still functioning about 1910 but it closed down soon afterwards and while W.H. had not made a fortune from it he does not seem to have lost much as he retained, by village standards, a prosperous life-style and was greatly respected as a genial, intelligent and honest man.

Nine days later, on December 23rd. 1904, another letter, which for its extraordinary range of news items and the light it throws on domestic and village life in those days deserves to be quoted almost fully. It begins with news of three other sea-going engineers.

> Jack the Mill has been here this morning asking David William to go for a walk with him. Hank is home again but Neville Evans wants him to take another trip in the Tampican and says that he'd have plenty of time before the Germanic will be ready . . . John was here on Wednesday, the day you were sailing, and it happened to be my 72nd birthday. God has been very good to me in giving me such a long life and good health for which I feel thankful.
>
> 5.30 p.m. The post has just brought us your post card from Palermo. It is a very good view I should think and you should be pleased to have such fine weather at Christmas. We are about sending Christmas gifts to Neta's children. David William is sending two scent bottles for the girls, got up in a pretty straw box, two bottles in each box and a board for Jack (Ring Quoits). Pincushion for Neta and half-quarter of tobacco for Hank . . .
>
> David William or myself will be going to Cardiff tomorrow for to fetch the turkey from John and on Christmas Day we shall be thinking of you. I must finish by wishing you a very happy Christmas and may you be lucky enough to spend next Christmas at home . . .

It is a comment on life-expectancy that on his 72nd. birthday the writer is expressing thankfulness for 'such a long life'. I am already ten years older and although few of my boyhood friends are left yet I am conscious of being surrounded by many of my own age and older. But to be over seventy in the early years of this century was an achievement worth noting.

51

Garfield, in middle age, as a Chief Engineer.

White Star Liner Olympic, sister ship of the ill-fated Titanic. In the early 1920s both Garfield and Wyndham Jones, also of Machen, were engineers together on the Olympic.

53

And our postal services of those days are vividly illuminated. He had just had a postcard from Palermo by the afternoon post at 5.30. And just two days before Christmas, December 23rd., they were about to send Christmas parcels to his daughter, son-in-law, and grandchildren at Liverpool, confident that they would be delivered there on Christmas Day, and I'm sure those children got their presents on Christmas Day. Nowadays we should be asked to allow two weeks, not two days.

That concentration on Christmas Eve or Christmas Day delivery persisted at least until the late 1920's. I was then living in a village about four miles from Abergavenny and knew well a fairly well-to-do family living in a large house that came within the round of the postman entrusted with the mail for outlying farms and cottages. On that Christmas morning the snow lay 'deep and even' and the day passed with the many children of the household in question watching for the postman. Dusk fell and still no post, whereupon the worried householder telephoned to the Head Postmaster at Abergavenny who confirmed that the postman had left for his round early and should have returned hours ago. Deeply concerned by this failure of His Majesty's mail to get through, he telephoned a few farms and found that while some had got their mail others hadn't. Eventually he contacted a farmhouse that could help him. The postman, his half-empty bags on the floor, was fast asleep before the kitchen fire and they couldn't wake him! To keep out the cold and to assist him in his arduous round through the snow the kind farmers had insisted that he had a glass of home-made wine or cider, possibly a whiskey or two—being Christmas—and the poor chap was flat out.

Dutifully, the Postmaster came out in his car picked up the bags (whether the postman also I can't remember) and nobly completed the round that Christmas night. He also said the postman would be sacked but the farmers, who felt a bit guilty, pleaded for him and I believe he won a reprieve. He was a nice chap and deservedly popular.

Four letters written in 1905 tell of the comings and goings of ships' engineers, all relations or friends, of the arrivals and departures of ships, and of accidents or illnesses suffered by friends and acquaintances. The father is pleased to announce that another son, David William, had been appointed Second Engineer on the Manxman, sailing from Bristol, via Antwerp to Portland, Oregon, at a wage of £13.10.0 with £1. bonus making £14.10.0 and adds 'Not bad is it?' That wage regarded by the father as very satisfactory, relates, of course to a month's hard and hazardous work, for he goes on to say that the voyage had begun in very rough weather.

In June 1905 a very sad entry reads: 'Poor Tom Holman died yesterday evening. They are now afraid his little sister is afflicted in the same way.' Two years earlier, in his first letter, the father had reported that John Holman and his wife were very poorly, with the wife not expected to live more than two or three months, and four months later he reported the death of John Holman. A year later, that is in the Spring of 1905 he mentioned that a son of the deceased, Tom Holman, 'has gone for a sea voyage to Constantinople for his health. He is very poorly.' In those days that could only mean tuberculosis. It was a killer, much dreaded in town and village. Young people in their teens seemed to be more at risk than younger children and older people and I lost several friends from it. For some young men a voyage on a cargo boat was despairingly accepted, when medicine could do no more, as offering some slight chance of escape, but it did not help in the case of young Tom Holman, nor did a voyage round the world in a cargo boat do so for William Spring, brother of the Cardiff-born novelist, Howard Spring, for, as related in his boyhood autobiography, 'Heaven Lies About Us', he died at sea.

Reading that letter I was reminded of the death in March 1918 of the writer's much loved grandson, John Davies, aged 25, from the same dreaded disease—or so it was said in the village at the time. He was a handsome young man. His brother, Trevor, two years younger, had predeceased him, in 1906, aged eleven years. Trevor's name appears only once in the extracts. In the last of the preserved letters, his grandfather wrote, 'Trevor received a p.c. from his uncle Hank at Algiers'. Trevor died just seven weeks later.

The last of the carefully treasured letters is dated 3rd January 1906. As with the first letter it contains a fascinating mixture of small news items. The Machen Cricket Club, which before the first World War, was one of the best in the county, was having a bazaar that day in the Boys' School, to be opened by Viscountess Hereford, and Jane is preparing to go. Albert Stephens had been home and 'telling us about meeting you in Italy'.

> The New Zealanders (that is the Rugby Football team) has been doing fine work in England, Ireland and Scotland but came to Wales to be beaten. I sent you some papers with the report of it . . .
>
> Thanks very much for your Christmas Card from Cape Town. We value it very much and will keep it as a souvenir of your first trip in the R.M.S. Athenic to New Zealand.

I believe the writer died soon afterwards as although I knew almost all the many characters mentioned by him he had departed from the scene a few years later when, aged about eight, I attended the wedding of the son, Garfield, with my aunt Laura in the Parish Church, which was a very grand affair indeed.

Garfield continued his sea-going career until his well earned retirement, serving in his later years as Chief Engineer on the prestigious transatlantic liners, and was on the liner Georgic when it was sunk by German bombers in the Suez Canal. All who knew him esteemed him highly, for he was a man of high principles, dedicated to doing what he saw to be his duty and utterly charming withal, who returned, in no small measure, the love shown to him by his father, as is amply demonstrated in the letters so carefully preserved through all the changes and chances of his life at sea.

Mrs. W. H. Davies, J.P. (Liz) when she was in her 70s.

MACHEN REVISITED

Commercial Road, Machen, c. 1900. (See key)

60

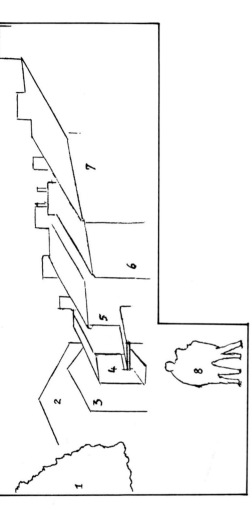

1. The 'conker tree': a delightful feature in the centre of the village. Felled 4th September 1969.

2. Siloam Baptist Chapel, erected 1837, demolished circa. 1975.

3. Meyricks' grocer's shop before removal a few years later to new premises opposite Siloam Chapel.

4. Hudson's grocer's shop.

5. Russell House, home and shop of W. H. Davies and his wife Elizabeth (Liz), son-in-law and daughter of David Stephens, who wrote the letters.

6. Home and shop of the said David Stephens, his daughter Jane (later second wife of G. D. Inkin, the village schoolmaster), and his sons David William, Abram and Garfield.

7. Manchester House, home and draper's shop of John Potter, his son, Ted (mentioned in the letters) and whose other sons and daughters contributed much to the life of the community.

8. Dr. Barnard, with his son, Gerald, near his surgery. Clad in breeches and stockings and riding a bicycle on his rounds, Dr. Barnard was a familiar figure at Machen over many years.

61

PORTRAITS OF THE VILLAGE

David Stephens's letters reveal a way of life in the first decade of this century so greatly at variance with life at Machen, and indeed, anywhere else in rural Wales, in the last quarter of this century as to make me wonder how so vast a change could have taken place within the span of my lifetime: I was born in 1902 and knew almost all the people he mentions. They disclose that village life ninety years ago was largely centered round what went on in its shops, chapels and pubs. They gave life and colour to the community and kept boredom at bay.

THE SHOPS

(The numbers in brackets relate to the key plan on previous page).

In 1912, I can recall at least 27 shops (and I might have overlooked some), most of which I entered at some time, when, as the eldest of four children, I was sent on shopping errands. They did more than supply food and clothes and pots and pans: they were meeting places where people lingered to exchange news and savour gossip, especially at Meyrick's store, where, in the summer of 1916, I was happy to work as an errand boy. It was then situated opposite Siloam chapel having moved there about six years earlier from a site almost opposite (No.3). In that earlier position it had been just two doors away from Hudson's (No.4), managed by a Mr. Hughes, which was next door to W.H. Davies's store (No.5) on the opposite corner of Alma Street. Thus there were three grocery stores, and all apparently doing well, within fifty yards of one another. But W.H. Davies was more than a grocer's; it was also a draper's—drapery on the left, foods on the right. W.H. Davies was David Stephens's son-in-law, and there is much about him, his wife Elizabeth (Liz.) and their many children in the letters.

62

Next door (No.7) was the home and shop of David Stephens, and (at that time) unmarried daughter, Jane, who managed the shop, until some years later she became the second wife of the village schoolmaster, Griffith Inkin. I remember that shop as being well stocked with all manner of goods in metals, glass and china. Rather surprisingly, having regard to her brother-in-law's grocer's shop next door, Jane sold at least one item of food—eggs. In a letter dated 3rd April 1904, David Stephens refers to his 'very fine lot of fowls, Orpingtons, Longshanks and Minorcas' and it can be assumed that the origin of this trade derived from a surplus of eggs over family requirements, but that source was supplemented by supplies from my grandmother's chickens at Nantygleisiad Farm. It sometimes fell to me to deliver those eggs, and I did so in baskets almost too heavy for me to carry to the shop more than a mile away. I'm sure grandmother never received a penny for them, the business being conducted by barter, eggs in exchange for the famous Wedgwood blue-and-white, jasper decorated porcelain, which Jane had always in stock. Thus my grandmother accumulated what would now be a very valuable collection of tea ware, jugs, vases and items for the dressing table, which, on marriage, she gave to her three daughters. I inherited some.

And if these three grocers were not enough for local demand, early in that first decade the Co-op opened a store and bakery on a site less than a hundred yards from the other three. It is hard to think of it as such now but in the early years of this century Machen was a shopping centre for the south end of the valley

As for the other trades, John Potter's Manchester House (No.7) was a draper's business, specialising , as its name suggests in cotton goods. In those days, women generally made their own dresses or employed a dressmaker to do so, and John Potter met that demand, selling haberdashery also.

In Lewis Street (more usually known in those days as Clay Street), Mrs. Martha Davies, a widow, had a milliner's business. She was the mother of Machen-trained Jack Davies, a sea-going engineer (but too young to be

Panoramic view of Upper Machen, circa. 1900.

·mentioned with others in the letters), who, as a chief engineer, gave distinguished service in the Merchant Navy throughout the second world war. She was the mother also of Annie, organist at Siloam chapel and a music teacher. Among her pupils was a very young boy from 1, Napier Street, who achieved distinction, even eminence, as a composer and organist in the U.S.A., Dr. Lyndon B. Salathiel, B.Mus., D.Litt., who in September 1990 completed fifty years as Minister of Music and organist, at the first Presbyterian Church at Pontiac, Michigan. He was a grandson of a local farmer, Sam Davies.

Another daughter, Hilda, taught at Machen School during the first world war, before marrying Bill Stephen of Ysgubor Fawr Farm, since completely built over. To their younger son, Bill, this work owes its existence as without his encouragement and support the letters would have remained unknown outside the family, as I have gratefully acknowledged elsewhere within these covers.

Another store that was always busy was the village post-office, then opposite the Ffwrwm Ishta inn. To buy stamps one passed through a small shop selling confectionary and stationery. The telephone had not come into general use and people relied on postcards, letters and telegrams for communication, and possibly no one in the area more than David Stephens. The postmaster, Ebrill Edwards, had other interests, as a composer and poet, which he pursued under the bardic name of Gwilym Lon. He left the counter business mainly to his faithful, long serving and able assistant, Violet Smith. I met Violet some forty or so years later when we attended a mayor-making ceremony at Chichester and the new mayor's reception afterwards. Violet was there because the new mayor was her nephew, the late Bill Pope, and I, by invitation, as a former Machen boy, who had known his parents and grandparents. Violet had also operated the small telephone exchange, taking telegrams through it, and on that happy occasion at Chichester she told me of the sorrow which that task had entailed, when during the first world war she took the telegrams informing next-of-kin that son or husband in the armed forces was 'missing' or killed. As the many names on the village war memorial attest, it was a duty that often fell to her.

Her father, William Smith of the Barracks, is mentioned twice in the letters, and in neither place to his advantage. On 15th. January, 1904, David Stephens wrote: 'Wm. Smith has not been for his exam. yet. He is going in a fortnight so he says. He has taken to drink and has a very foul mouth.' When I remember him, as a fellow engineer with my father at the railway works, he had given up the sea, and, I believe, alcohol—at least I never recall his being drunk—but not his foul mouth and ill temper. As a side-line he had a small bicycle business, repairing and hiring out bicycles and tandems, and it was on his hired cycles that I learned to ride. Once, I had to return a cycle punctured and though it was not my fault I returned it with fear and trembling. Seeing Bill Smith in his garden I dropped the cycle at his gate and ran; I did not want to hear what he thought of me. It all went to make life at Machen eventful. In the second mention, some six weeks later, he is said to be 'still idle'. That meant 'unemployed'—not lazy. William Smith was never indolent.

CHURCHES AND CHAPELS

David Stephens's account of the electrifying effect of the Evan Roberts's revival meetings in Ebenezer chapel conveys vividly the impact made on the village by that extraordinary religious experience, though he does not appear to have attended any. Almost all his letters bear testimony of the extent to which religious interest and attendance at worship gave meaning and colour to the lives of many Machen people ninety years ago. For him, attendance at the Wesleyan Methodist chapel would have been not a duty but a looked-forward-to pleasure, as it was to my paternal grandfather, Herbert Jones.

My own attendance there was also a pleasure, one hard to imagine nowadays. My grandfather died in 1911, after some months of illness, so it must have been about 1910 that he took me, then aged eight, and sometimes, my younger brother, Gwyn, with him to that same chapel on Sunday mornings. Clad in sailor suits, our hands clasped in his, we walked happily with him to his front pew in what, in that cruciform chapel, would be the south transept, where, small as we were, we had a good view of all that went on, including Ernest Meyrick at the American organ, only a few feet away, and leading the singing as he pumped and played.

In the row behind were David Stephens's youngest grand-daughters, the fair and beautiful (and not only in my adoring young eyes) Evelyn, Rosalie and Anita, and, of course, their parents, but I have forgotten their presence there. How I wished they had been in front of me! I would willingly have sacrificed the sight of Ernest at the organ for that pleasure! And then the walk home, stopping sometimes for Grandpa to call on 'old Mr. Newton', the Crimean war veteran in his cottage opposite the chapel, his army medals over the mantelpiece testifying to his part in that campaign fifty years earlier. That was grandpa: kind, generous and good neighbourly, whose interest in the careers of the engineering apprentices trained under him at the railway workshops gave him lasting pleasure, especially when, like Garfield Stephens, they did well.

On his death our chapel going was switched to Siloam, the larger of the two Baptist chapels, where we shared the pew of our maternal grandmother. Her husband, Arthur Knight Thomas, a painfully shy and reserved man, never attended: even at funerals he avoided going inside the church.

I have written about that chapel-going and the effects I think it had on my life in His Lordship's Obedient Servant* and will mention here only two experiences, not touched on in those memoirs, which etched themselves deeply on my consciousness.

The first was the marriage of Garfield and my aunt, Laura, in the parish church of St. Michael, on 4th February 1909, an event which, 82 years later, I can still

* Published 1987 by Gomer Press, £7.95

recall vividly because it was a grand occasion. I was in my seventh year, and my brother, Gwyn, who was with me, in his fifth. There were the carriages with their white beribboned horses, my smiling grandfather who gave away the bride (her father having died when she and her sister, Rose, were very young), Garfield happy and resplendent in full morning dress and Laura a magnificently gowned bride. I can't remember how Gwyn and I got to the church but I have not forgotten the return journey to the bride's home. Abram (Garfield's brother) packed Gwyn and me into one of the carriages along with his bulky self and several other adults, and off we trotted until, near the lime kilns, we were held up by a rope across the road held by men who demanded tribute, which Abram cheerfully forked out, before we were allowed to pass. I had witnessed the old custom of chain-a-wedding.

The other experience had less relevance to the Machen that David Stephens knew, as it happened in 1915, nine years after his death, but it was a pointer to the changes that were to transform the village into the one that now exists. For, as I noted in my running commentary on the letters, the Wesleyan chapel which he and his family loved and supported, together with Siloam, the Baptist chapel, supported very generously by my Thomas grandmother, and Adullam, the Congregational chapel, so sedulously sustained over many years by David Stephens's future son-in-law, the village schoolmaster, Griffith Inkin, all have disappeared, leaving only Ebenezer, the smaller of the two Baptist chapels, a loss made up only in part by a Pentecostalist Hall to serve a sect that established itself in the village just before the outbreak of the first world war.

On a winter night (I think in 1915 when I was 13) sent with my friend Wally Williams to attend a chapel and not being able to agree on whether to attend his family's chapel, Adullam, or mine, Siloam, we rashly decided to try the Pentecostalists, known to us then only as the 'second-comers' because of their belief in the imminent second coming of Christ.

Their Sunday evening services were held in Nantygleisiad Cottage, home of Edward Thomas, of whom I have written in His Lordship's Obedient Servant. It was a cold night but the blazing fire in the living room and the ten or so others present generated a comfortable warmth even near the door where Wally and I were told to sit. I had not been seated long before I became uncomfortable: I felt that attention was being focussed on us and that we were about to be grilled. A young woman, known to me as almost illiterate, spoke 'in tongues' which the preacher (a local insurance agent) professed to understand, as, with face uplifted and eyes closed, he interjected from time to time, 'Yes, Lord!', 'Praise the Lord!', 'Hallelujah!'. But he made no attempt to interpret.

His ranting form of preaching was interspersed with full throated hymn singing and my discomfort increased: I was paying for daring to enter this den. The overcrowded room, the blazing fire and a hanging oil lamp near the preacher's head caused streams of sweat to pour from his forehead. And I sweated too, as the preacher went on to pray long and fervently for the conversion of the two young sinners who had been led into their midst that night. The pressure to declare ourselves converted was almost intolerable and I wondered what would happen if, being close to the door, we made a bolt for it. Stubbornly we held out. Released at last into the cold night air, Wally and I breathed deeply and thankfully as Wally remarked, 'My father would have given me a hell of a thrashing if I'd become a second comer'.

That this sect, despised and rejected by the 'respectable' church and chapel-goers should have established itself firmly in that community while the chapels of some of those who despised them are no longer there has led me to think that the Pentecostalists, with their enthusiasm, have met a need that the older churches seemed powerless to provide. Had this happened in the context of a declining population it would be less surprising, but geographically at least, Machen is now twice the size of the Machen I knew.

THE PUBS

Of the pubs I have less to say as I knew them only from the outside. Many years were to pass before youths and young men from 'respectable' families would frequent them. Girls and ladies never entered them, but occasionally a shawled woman hiding a jug might be seen coming from a 'Bottle and Jug' hatch, a facility provided by many inns, with beer for her husband's—and possibly her own— supper. The pubs were for men only. (Having said that I am wondering whether the group of ladies shown outside the rather remote Maenllwyd Inn in the photograph opposite on page 71 went inside or had a pot of tea brought out to them.)

Machen pubs were then places where men drank beer (which was very cheap), cursed loudly, exchanged bawdy stories, argued, quarrelled and fought. Sometimes, especially on Saturday nights, the often bloody fights spilled out into the road and were very frightening to me as a timid twelve-year-old.

Sixty years passed before I mustered enough courage to enter a Machen pub, such was my childhood dread of them, and then only as a result of a strange, direct invitation to come inside. In the meantime, I had grown to enjoy pub meals, with wine or beer, in the area where I live on the Hampshire-Sussex border. In 1978, however, on a visit to my brother Gwyn at Nantygleisiad Farm, my way on foot from a bus stop took me past the Forge Hammer and White Hart inns. Approaching them, I recalled letters (now in Newport Museum) written by my great grand-father in 1865, when, as a civil engineer, he was respons-ible for the conversion of the old tram road into the Brecon and Merthyr Railway, and for the construction of the loop line between Machen and Caerphilly. These works had the effect of isolating the hamlet of White Hart, with its two inns and few houses from the main road, thus depriving both pubs of an important source of trade. That was not all; the pubs were dealt a double blow, since it was here that the men and horses employed on the tram road had a main stopping place, possibly the last before Newport and the

Ladies outside the Maenllwyd Inn, apparently interested but not daring to go inside.

The Hope and Anchor Inn, Shirehampton, near Bristol. The home and business of David William Stephens from 1919 until his death in 1937, whose figure can be dimly seen in the doorway and that of his wife, with one of their nine children, in a bedroom window.

71

first out of it. It was where the hauliers rested, fed and watered their horses and had them shod, and where they, too, rested, fed and drank. Naturally, the innkeepers protested and in these letters my great-grandfather was explaining to the company's directors what had happened and the effects that were to follow.

Stimulated by that memory (I had discovered the letters only a year or so earlier), I stopped outside the Forge Hammer and looked at it with special interest. It was mid-day in summer and I was hot, tired and thirsty. I longed to go in, not only for a refreshing glass of beer but also because of my great-grandfather's references to the place and the damage he had perforce done to its trade. But these inducements were countered as memories of Saturday night drunkenness and brawling there flooded into my consciousness. Leaning on my stick in the road outside, torn by indecision, a cheerful middle-aged man appeared at the door and jocularly beckoned to me to come inside. I have a feeling that he did not expect me to accept. Nevertheless, he generously insisted on paying for my sandwich and beer. The long-held fear and prejudice had been broken. I had been a stranger to them all, but the warmth of welcome, combined with the rest and refreshment, set me up for the walk through the fields: but I never took it, as the landlord, discovering where I was bound, got out his car and drove me by the lane to the farm.

Two years later, on another visit, I was bolder. After a walk on the mountain path I had trod on my way to and from school at Risca sixtyfive years earlier, to the bar of Ffwrwm Ishta inn for a ploughman's lunch, with beer, where again I felt grateful for the metamorphosis that had transformed at least two of Machen's sordid beerhouses, with spit and sawdust bars, into inns serving good food and drink (not necessarily alcoholic) in clean and pleasant conditions, accompanied by courtesy and friendliness.

At a Machen Carnival, c. 1910, or Coronation procession 1911. Ebrill Edwards, postmaster, on box seat, Cornelius Roberts, farmer and landlord of the Ffwrwm Ishta Inn, in tweeds and cap, and Griffith Inkin, schoolmaster, at rear. Coachman, Mat. Matthews.

73

Another feature of village life in those days was the barber's shop. At fifteen I began shaving, and, for a year or so, used with difficulty a 'cut-throat' razor. My first safety razor was an American army Gillette given to me by my uncle Wyndham, who, in 1919 was employed as an engineer on the White Star liner, R.M.S. Olympic, then engaged in returning American troops back to the U.S.A. after the war. With few houses having running water indoors, and so many men having to shave by lamplight or candlelight, a large proportion of them relied on the barber to shave them once or twice a week. My father was one of them.

At Machen before the first world war, this need was met by a Mr. Gamble. His saloon was well-kept and well patronised as the dozens of private mugs on his shelves testified, each mug with its own brush and piece of soap and bearing a consecutive number in bold figures. Looking at them when having my hair cut, I asked Mr. Gamble which was my father's. He gave a number somewhere in the region of 80. This was an hygenic measure to reduce the risk of barber's rash—a common condition at that time.

Soon after the war began Mr. Gamble left, possibly for war service, and the village was left without a barber. My father reverted to his old cut-throat razor and went without the luxury of being shaved in the company of men with whom to exchange news and gossip. And I had to go elsewhere for my haircutting. I did not have to look far. Next door to John Potter's Manchester House shop was a sweet shop kept by a jolly young woman, May Jones, who shared the house behind it with her bachelor brother, known to all by his christian names only, William Henry, by day, a mason working for the Tredegar Estate and, at night, as a barber in a back room, approached by a steep flight of brick or stone steps, unlit and rather dangerous.

Anything more primitive would be hard to imagine. Three backless benches and a wooden arm chair, in which the victim sat, constituted the furniture. Ablutions were left to the shaven if he did not mind using the facilities provided, which consisted of a bowl of cold water with a floating sponge set on a bench near the door on which hung a roller towel. There was no running water. In winter, a coal fire burned in the grate before which William Henry worked in the light of a small oil lamp with a reflector back, set on the mantelpiece, which gave him just enough light to avoid cutting off someone's nose. The rest of the room was in shadow.

To that shack my friend and second cousin, Jack Rees (a grandson of John Potter) on a winter's night in 1916, where we sat awaiting our turn. William Henry was a splendid teller of tales, usually comic, some slightly scandalous and all interesting about people he had met, worked with or heard of. He thus provided excellent entertainment and a long wait imposed no hardship in spite of the rough benches on which one sat.

That night, among those waiting, were two men who, when not engaged in poaching, worked as miners, aged, I think, about thirty. I knew them well and their reputation. One or both had recently been prosecuted for poaching on Lord Tredegar's estate, and the talk was of injustice and unreasonableness on the part of the magistrates. That subject exhausted, their talk took a more interesting turn—about women. The discussion had only just begun when one of the poachers realising that Jack and I were taking a great interest, stopped talking, winked at William Henry and nodded towards us. William Henry got the message, and, turning to me, said 'Come on nipper, I'll do you next'. He did so. Holding my head firmly in his big mason's hand he took the clippers, and , beginning at the nape of my neck, went over the top and came out in the middle of my forehead. He dealt similarly with both sides of the initial swathe so that in less than a minute I was 'done', and paying a penny or twopence, waited for Jack. He was treated likewise, and when I saw the result I saw what I looked like. My mother and father were appalled: I was the first 'skinhead' they had seen. My father said, 'I'll have a word with William Henry about this', but I knew he wouldn't. He liked William Henry—everyone did—and

75

William Henry, always cheerful and carefree, would have just smiled and responded with the 'soft answer that turneth away wrath'.

I was a little late for my first class at Pontywaun County School next morning, and the lesson had begun when I quietly opened the door, hoping to get to my desk in the front row while the teacher, a woman, busy at the blackboard, had her back to the class. Unfortunately, the door was in a front corner of the room, and as soon as I appeared a roar of laughter greeted the shorn head. I recall the teacher turning round swiftly and the rising anger in her countenance melting into laughter as she caught sight of me. That roar of laughter remained painfully in my consciousness until I had grown a fresh crop of hair. After that I was sent by train into Newport whenever my hair needed cutting.

Precisely seventy years later having business to transact with the publisher of His Lordship's Obedient Servant I went down to Llandysul in Dyfed which involved an overnight stay in a local hotel. Failing to complete our business at an afternoon appointment, another meeting was fixed for eleven o'clock the following morning. Leaving the hotel about ten o'clock in a slight drizzle I resolved to see inside the ancient church and explore the town. But the church was locked and the drizzle had become heavy rain. Further exploration was ruled out. But what was I to do for almost an hour? The pubs were shut. I decided to have my hair cut, believing that if I had to wait my turn it would be in the company of other men, whose conversation I might enjoy, though in that Welsh-speaking area, I might be looked upon as a foreigner. At the lower end of the main street I soon found a Unisex Hairdressing Salon, with a woman in full view of the street having a 'hairdo'. That was no place for me and in the now heavy rain I trudged up one side of the long street and down the other until I came again to the Unisex salon having failed to find a men-only establishment. I had to get out of that rain and, with some daring, I went in. The proprietress was just finishing off the woman, and, saying she would 'do' me, told me to sit in a chair alongside while a very young girl assistant made a start on me. I was thankful that no one I knew would be likely to see me through that large window. After a few minutes the boss came to 'finish me off'.

I noted that she had been speaking in Welsh to the woman customer but I was puzzled by her curious accent when speaking to me in English. A north Walian, I said to myself, a guess that seemed confirmed by her Mediterranean features and colouring, so often seen among the swarthy folk of north Wales. Her friendly nature encouraged me to ask where she came from. 'Pontypridd',she said. 'And before that?' 'Calabria.' 'So you are an Italian.' 'Yes, I am Italian.'

I was driven back to Carmarthen station by a middle-aged man, a native of Llandysul, and I told him of my failure to find a men's hairdresser in the town. 'There isn't one,' he said.

The contrast between that experience and my boyhood visits to William Henry's establishment is so vast that it is hard to believe such change has taken place in rural Wales within the span of my lifetime.

LIFE AND DEATH

In his letter of 23rd December 1904, David Stephens congratulates himself on his longevity: 'God has been very good to me in giving me such a long life and good health for which I feel thankful.' He was then 72 and died early in May 1906, just eighteen months later, and was buried at Machen.

For me, now in my 90th year, whose mother died in 1979 in her 102nd year and her sister, Lillie, a few years later, aged 100, and brother, John, who is in his 96th year as I write, to die at 73 is untimely young.

These figures illustrate what perhaps has been the most significant change of all—that of life expectancy. The change is made clearly manifest when we look at some of the dates shown in his family tree, where I found that a much loved grandson, Trevor, a child of his daughter, Liz., living next door, died in February 1906, aged 11, just two months before David Stephens's own death. That must have been a grievious blow to him and might have hastened his decease.* He was spared the sorrow of the long illness and death of Trevor's brother, John, in March 1918, aged 25, whom I remember as a cheerful and good looking young man.

Two of David Stephens's own sons did not attain old age, John dying in 1910, aged 45, and Abram in 1919, aged 56, both unmarried.

The many references to illness and deaths in the village might be taken as indicating that Machen was an unhealthy place at that time: I believe the contrary to be true. That was what life was like in all of rural Gwent, and much worse in west Wales where tuberculosis was said to be even more prevalent.

In the years of which I write our lives at Machen were very much in the hands of Dr. Barnard, a little man who spoke with a strange accent, suggesting a foreign origin. My father said he was a French Jew, and I have no doubt that he was Jewish: he was never known to have attended church or chapel. He was kind and gentle and much respected, and I am sure did his best with the limited resources science had then placed in his hands. I recall entering his surgery a number of times, usually for bottles of medicines for others. There were three kinds—white, pink and brown, dispensed behind a heavy curtain. I remember going to him for myself only twice: once after I had foolishly lost the tip of a finger in a piece of farm machinery in which I should never have put it. The other occasion was when a raging toothache sent me to him asking him to take it out; wisely he refused to touch it—it would have been without any form of anaesthesia.

The surgery was almost as primitive as William Henry's

---

*This conjecture concerning the effect of Trevor's death on his fond grandfather has since been reinforced by Mrs. Susan Ward, a daughter of Evelyn, who was a year younger. Mrs. Ward has told me that he died tragically by falling from a carriage and being run over by its wheels. His death was instantaneous.

barber's shop. The waiting room was in the open air in front of a side door set in a draughty passage between the doctor's house and that of Garfield's mother-in-law, my great-aunt Bella. Here in all weathers one waited one's turn. On the wall of the surgery there may have been several pictures, but I remember only one: a large, coloured, glossy depiction of a compound fracture of the shin bone, with several inches of shin bone protruding through a wound, dripping with very red blood. I would look at it with horrified fascination. Had Dr. Barnard been dishonest I might have thought he had snitched it from a medical school as it was mounted on linen, with two wooden rolls like the pictures on the walls of our new school (built 1908). Perhaps dealing with wounds was his speciality, as injuries in the local works and collieries were very frequent.

When eighty years later I attend our local health centre, with its warm and comfortable waiting rooms, with magazines for old and young and those in between, its diagnostic aids and teams of receptionists and nurses, I sometimes grimly recall Dr. Barnards surgery and his hit-or-miss diagnoses. But he was very professional and, as I have said, did his best.

Some years after my family left Machen, his place was taken by two young doctors, both of whom married grand-daughters of David Stephens. They were the very attractive youngest daughters of Liz: Rosalie to Dr. Ivor Morgan, who, I have been told, left no children, and Anita to Dr. Cecil Davies, which union produced two sons, one of whom, I understand , also became a doctor.

CRIME

Of crime at Machen I have little to say; few crimes were committed and none that I can recall was serious.

There was, of course, much drunkenness which, if not accompanied by disorderliness, was tolerated. Fights inside and outside pubs, usually on Saturday nights, oftentimes bloody, were usually over before Police Constable Morgan made his leisurely way towards them.

Poaching, though officially a crime—or certainly an indictable offence—was endemic and could not be eradicated: Lord Tredegar's coverts and woods were too conveniently near. Not only the poachers but also a number of otherwise law abiding people believed that pheasants and rabbits were God given benefits for everyone to enjoy, some in the hunt for them and others at the table. The fact that most pheasants taken had been hand reared was held to be irrelevant, if considered at all.

Of criminal sex offences I remember none, though that is not the same as saying there weren't any. Certainly, women and girls could go anywhere—in the fields, woods, lanes or on the mountain—without fear of molestation.

As for robberies and burglaries, I recall only an attempted break-in. Our home was within sixty yards of the railway station, and lying in bed half awake about six o'clock on a Sunday morning in summer, I was startled by the sound of breaking glass, followed a moment or so later by the shout of 'burglars' from a man running past the house. I guessed what had happened. There had been a number of early Sunday morning break-ins at the station booking offices in the area, the spoil being the heavy Saturday takings. Expecting Machen to become a target, the Brecon and Merthyr Railway Company appointed a night watchman. I knew the man well—he was the father of my friend, Jack Rees—and I could not think of a man less suited for the job of security guard. When the large brick came through the window he was not merely startled, he was terrified, and, forsaking the property he was being paid to protect, ran shouting 'burglars!' to the home of his boss Jimmy Williams, foreman at the railway works, who was asleep. By the time Jimmy Williams had dressed the would-be robber was beyond risk of pursuit as he headed up the steep lane that led over the mountain where his home was thought to be.

I was to hear that shout of 'burglars!' a year or so later. Again I was in bed, knowing that sleep would be impossible until the 10 o'clock Saturday night train from

Newport (The Rodney) had departed after delivering its usual load of drunks and revellers, always accompanied by the slamming of carriage doors, a shrill engine whistle and shouts of friendly abuse and farewell. That night, shortly after the hubbub had ceased and I was settling myself down for sleep, I became aware of a commotion in front of the house, and my mother and father talking excitedly downstairs. I went down to find what was happening. My mother said 'There are burglars in Adullam chapel'. I wasn't going to miss this, and dressing quickly, joined the small crowd that had gathered at the back of the chapel (long since demolished) which stood at the corner of Wyndham Street and Lewis (Clay) Street, with its back almost opposite our front windows: there was another group in Lewis Street. Even then I could not imagine burglars in Adullam chapel: I could not think of anything in it worth stealing. Still, a man off the ten o'clock train had seen a momentary flicker of light, as if a match had been struck, as he passed a window. Perhaps he had been drinking, like most of the others off the train.

Suddenly, a shout of 'It's a woman!' from the people around me. And indeed it was. In the darkness the figure of a woman was dimly outlined, perched precariously on the ridge of the roof of the chapel schoolroom, apparently trying to make her way to a bedroom of an empty cottage adjoining. Realising she had been seen the distraught woman returned with difficulty to the chapel through the gallery window through which she had made her bid to escape. She was the chapel caretaker. The excitement over, I was ordered back to bed.

A day or so later, pretending to be absorbed in a book I was reading, I heard my parents and some other grown-ups discussing the incident, and learnt that there had been a man with her in the chapel, a man I knew well, the father of children of about my age and an officer of some sort in the chapel. That being so I could easily, at that age, have surmised that the two were together on some chapel business, but why in the dark? From slight gaps in the conversation, filled by a nod or a wink, which I sensed rather than saw, it became clear to me that the grown-ups

81

interpreted the situation differently. Be that as it may, what the couple were up to in the chapel did not, I think, rank as a criminal offence.

The cottage to which the poor frightened woman tried to make her perilous way had been recently vacated by a local miners' leader, known to me and other children in the village as 'Jackass Thomas', or, more familiarly, just 'Jackass', which I thought disrespectful. Years later, I realized that, as was the custom in Wales, with its legions of Joneses, Davieses, Evanses, and Thomases, he was being referred and addressed to his face by his first name and the initial of his second name, 'Jack S.', just as William Henry was seldom known by his surname of Jones. The cottage was later occupied by an elderly widow, as were the other two in the terrace. A few years after the chapel incident, neighbours and others in the street, noting that the old woman in the middle cottage had not been seen

The old Police Station Machen, with lock-up in the foreground and P.C. Morgan in the garden. 1905.

or heard for several days became alarmed. Knocking on her door producing no response, a group of women gathered outside and discussed what ought to be done. A front bedroom window being slightly open they decided on gaining entry by a ladder. A ladder was found and a young man cajoled into using it: he did not relish the job. Still, with all those women looking to him to do something! With the women looking on anxiously he disappeared into the bedroom, but only momentarily, and instead of descending the ladder rung by rung, he slid down it, white-faced and obviously scared. 'Is she alive?' a woman enquired in a voice hardly more than a whisper. He replied in a manner typical of a young South Walian, 'Yes, and bloody well kicking!' With that, the woman believed to have been dead appeared at the window shaking her fist and heaping imprecations on the crowd below, now convulsed with relief and laughter.

This was the Machen when David Stephens wrote those letters and I grew up, for it did not change until after the first world war. I have never regretted that I was born and spent my early life there: a lively community in a beautiful natural setting, a place of comedy and tragedy, of laughter and tears. Never of boredom.

Likewise, while I was conscious of much goodness in those among whom I lived, I was aware also of some wickedness, to which, alas, I think I contributed more than my fair share. In 1980, aged 78, I revisited Machen, staying with my brother, Gwyn, at Nantygleisiad Farm, where we had spent much of our boyhood. In the course of that visit he took me to call on Mrs. Violet Lewis, née Woodruff (since deceased), a widow in her early eighties. We had not seen each other for sixty years and I remembered her as a very attractive and highly intelligent girl, two or three years older than myself, who later taught in the village school. She belonged to a respected local family, being the grand-daughter of Philip Woodruff, who had lived at Y Fedw and owned the old Machen tinplate works, which a hundred years earlier had employed more than two hundred. Gwyn had told me that Mrs. Lewis, much liked and greatly respected, would be pleased to see me, and remembering her, her parents, two brothers, and sister Avice, I looked forward to the meeting.

She also remembered me. On introducing me Gwyn had said, 'This is my brother, Arthur!'. Shaking hands in welcome, Mrs. Lewis said, 'Yes, I remember you as the worst boy in the village!'.

So in reporting the follies and misdeeds of others I have not been unmindful of my own.

A class at Machen School in 1918 or 1919. The condition of some of the children speaks of wartime food shortage and hardship. With the headmaster, Griffith D. Inkin, are a pupil teacher, Brenda Stephen (who died a year or so later), and another teacher, Hilda Davies (later Mrs. William Stephen of Ysgubor Fawr Farm). The well nourished boy at the left end of the front row is Norman Stephens, Garfield's elder son, who went on to Lewis's School, Pengam and Southampton University.